Usborne Beginners
Dogs

Emma Helbrough
Designed by Josephine Thompson

Illustrated by Patrizia Donaera and Uwe Mayer

Dog consultant: Emma Milne

Reading consultant: Alison Kelly
Roehampton University of Surrey

SCHOLASTIC INC.

New York   Toronto   London   Auckland   Sydney
Mexico City   New Delhi   Hong Kong   Buenos Aires

Contents

Different dogs

There are lots of different kinds of dogs.
Some are very big, but others are tiny.
They can have long fur or short fur.

This spotted dog is
called a Dalmatian.

Puppies

Mother dogs usually give birth to between six and ten puppies. They sleep close together to keep warm.

A group of puppies is called a litter.

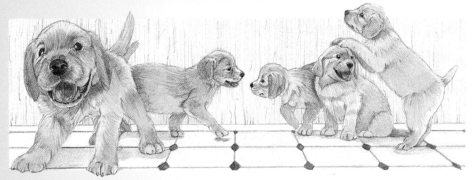

Puppies begin to walk at two weeks old.
They like to explore as they get older.

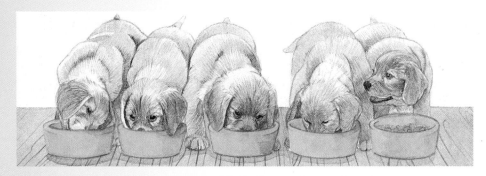

Puppies grow their first teeth at three
weeks old and begin to eat solid food.

They start to grow their adult teeth at four
months old and like to chew things.

Playtime

Puppies start to play together when they are about three weeks old.

Puppies like to play-fight. They jump on top of each other to show who is strongest.

Dogs often chase each other around parks. They take turns being chased.

Some dogs live in the wild. Wolves are wild dogs. Their pups play like pet puppies.

 Pet puppies chase after things for fun.

 Wild pups chase too but they are learning to hunt.

In the pack

Dogs like to be with people or other dogs.

Wolves live in groups called packs.

There can be up to fifteen wolves in a pack. One of the wolves is the pack leader. The other wolves follow their leader's orders.

Pet dogs think their owner is their pack leader.

A dog greets its pack leader by lick-ing its face.

Then it lies on its back to show it knows who is boss.

Puppies often play as if they are in a pack.

One of the puppies is always more bossy than the rest. It acts as the pack leader.

On guard

A dog's home and the area around it is called its territory.

Dogs think they own their territory, so they guard it.

They bark when strangers come near.

Basenjis are the only kind of dog that can't bark.

Dogs wet
around their
territory to leave
their smell behind.

When a dog sniffs an area it can tell if it
belongs to another dog.

Dogs try to take over each other's territory.

A dog sniffs a post
where another dog
has already been.

Then it wets the
post to cover up the
other dog's smell.

Dog talk

Dogs make lots of noises but they use their face and body to show how they feel too.

A dog wags its tail quickly when it is happy or excited.

It growls and shows its teeth when it is very angry.

It pricks its ears up when it is interested in something.

It puts its tail between its legs if it thinks it is in trouble.

WOOO

Some dogs howl if they are left alone. They are calling to their owner.

This dog wants to play. It has put its front legs down and its bottom in the air.

This is called a play-bow.

Digging

Dogs like to dig for fun but they dig for lots of other reasons too.

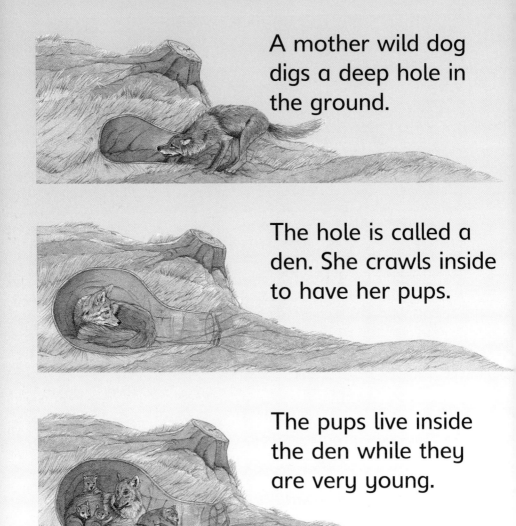

A mother wild dog digs a deep hole in the ground.

The hole is called a den. She crawls inside to have her pups.

The pups live inside the den while they are very young.

On a hot day, some dogs dig a hole in the ground.

Then they lie in the hole because it's cooler there.

Dogs often bury their toys to keep them safe. They dig them up when they want to play.

In the wild

Wild dogs hunt for food in packs. Their young pups stay behind in the den.

These African wild dog pups are waiting for their pack to return from hunting.

African wild dogs live in hot places, so they spend most of the day resting in the shade.

On a hunt, a pack of African wild dogs creeps up on a group of zebras.

The zebras scatter when they see the dogs. The dogs begin to chase one of the zebras.

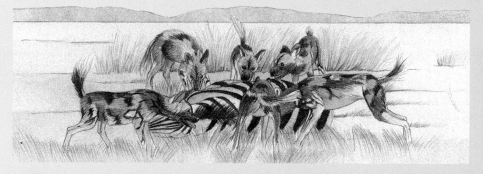

When the zebra gets tired, the dogs catch it and gather around to eat it.

Sniffing around

Dogs have an amazing sense of smell. They can tell more about something by smelling it than by looking at it.

Dogs sniff each other when they meet.

They can tell how old another dog is and if it's a male or a female just by sniffing it.

After a dog has been given a bath, its fur smells different.

So it rolls in smelly things to cover up the new smell.

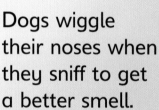

Dogs wiggle their noses when they sniff to get a better smell.

Bloodhounds have the best sense of smell. It is thousands of times better than yours.

Search and rescue

Dogs use their good sense of smell to help people find things and find other people.

At airports trained dogs sniff people's bags.

They find things that people are not allowed to take on planes, such as animals and weapons.

After an earthquake dogs help rescue teams search through the rubble.

Rescue teams use dogs to find people who are lost on mountains.

A dog can smell if someone is trapped under the snow.

The dog barks when it finds someone and the team digs them out.

21

Clever helpers

Some dogs are trained to help people who can't hear or see very well.

Hearing dogs tell their owner if they hear a sound, such as an alarm clock.

The dog touches its owner with a paw when it hears a sound.

If it hears a smoke alarm, the dog lies down to show danger.

If it hears a doorbell, the dog then leads its owner to the door.

Guide dogs help people who can't see well to travel safely.

The dogs are trained to lead their owner around things.

They learn to wait at the edge of a road until it is safe to cross.

Sheepdogs

Farmers use dogs to round up sheep in fields.

A kind of dog called a border collie is often used as a sheepdog.

This puppy will start training to be a sheepdog when it is six months old.

Sheepdogs can also be trained to round up cows, goats and even ducks!

The farmer uses a whistle and shouts to the sheepdog.

The sheepdog creeps behind the sheep and guides them to a sheep pen.

If a sheep strays from the group, the sheepdog runs over to guide it back again.

Sled dogs

Teams of dogs pull sleds across the snow. Some people use them to travel around. Other people race them for fun.

Each dog wears a harness which clips onto a long line.

Then the line is joined to the front of the sled.

The person who drives the sled is called a musher.

Sled dogs get hungry after running a race.
They eat six times as much food as pet dogs.

The dogs often wear socks to protect their paws from the snow.

The musher shouts "hike" or "let's go" to start the dogs.

Dog families

If a mother and a father dog look exactly the same, their puppies look the same too. They are called purebreds.

These old English sheepdog puppies will grow up to look like their parents.

If a mother and a father dog don't look the same...

...their puppies look like a mixture of both of them.

Dogs that are a mixture of different kinds are called mixed breeds.

Mixed breed dogs are often more healthy and live longer than purebred dogs.

Glossary of dog words

Here are some of the words in this book you might not know. This page tells you what they mean.

 pups - another word for puppies. Wild dog puppies are often called pups.

 pack - a group of dogs. Wild dogs live in packs.

 pack leader - the dog that is in charge of all the other dogs in a pack.

 territory - the place where a dog lives. Dogs guard their territory.

 den - the place where wild pups are born and live when they are very small.

 harness - a special strap that a dog sometimes wears.

 sheepdog - a dog that is trained to round up sheep.

Websites to visit

If you have a computer, you can find out more about dogs on the Internet. On the Usborne Quicklinks Website there are links to four fun websites.

Website 1 - Learn how to draw a puppy.

Website 2 - Make dog masks, cards and puppets.

Website 3 - Print pictures of different kinds of dogs to fill in.

Website 4 - Find out more about dogs.

To visit these websites, go to **www.usborne-quicklinks.com** and type the keywords "beginners dogs". Then, click on the link for the website you want to visit. Before you use the Internet, look at the safety guidelines inside the back cover of this book and ask an adult to read them with you.

Index

Acknowledgements

Managing editor: Fiona Watt,
Managing designer: Mary Cartwright
Photographic manipulation: John Russell

Photo credits

The publishers are grateful to the following for permission to reproduce material.
© **Africa Imagery:** 16 (Roger de la Harpe); © **Ardea:** 11, 24 (John Daniels);
© **Frank Lane Picture Agency:** 8 (Tim Fitzharris/Minden Pictures), 23 (Klein/Hubert/FotoNatura);
© **Getty:** cover, 29 (Patricia Doyle), 1 (Gary Randall), 2-3 (Geoff du Feu), 19 (Dag Sundberg);
© **ImageState:** 28; © **Leeson Photos:** 7 (Tom & Pat Leeson); © **NHPA:** 4 (E.A. Janes)
9 (Henry Ausloos); © **Powerstock:** 21 (Bob Winsett/Index Stock Imagery);
© **Richard Schiller:** 26-27; © **Warren Photographic:** 6, 10, 18, 31 (Jane Burton),
13 (Kim Taylor); © **Workbookstock:** 15 (Lori Adamski-Peek).

Usborne Beginners
Cats

Anna Milbourne
Designed by Michelle Lawrence
Illustrated by Patrizia Donaera and Christyan Fox

Cat consultant: Claire Bessant

Reading consultant: Alison Kelly
University of Surrey Roehampton

SCHOLASTIC INC.
New York Toronto London Auckland Sydney
Mexico City New Delhi Hong Kong Buenos Aires

Contents

A new family

A mother cat finds a warm, safe place to have her kittens.

The kittens are born. One by one, the mother cat licks them clean.

Growing up

New kittens cuddle up to their mother to keep warm.

They sleep most of the time.

A mother cat has six teats on her tummy. Her kittens suck them to drink her milk.

Kittens are born with their eyes shut. After about ten days, they open their eyes.

About two weeks later, they learn to walk. This kitten is taking its first steps.

They grow teeth and start to eat meat. Soon, they stop drinking milk.

All kittens have blue eyes to begin with.
Later, they can turn green or yellow or orange.

Playing

Kittens like to play. They learn how to do things by playing games.

These kittens are play-fighting.

They won't really hurt each other.

Grown-up pet cats like to play, too. It stops them from getting bored.

Kittens pretend to hunt. A kitten creeps up to its mother's tail.

It pounces and catches the tail with its paws.

Some kittens live in the wild, like this lynx. It likes to play too, but it will have to hunt and fight for real when it grows up.

Leaving home

To make good pets, kittens have to get used to people before they are eight weeks old.

Kittens learn to be friendly by copying their mother.

If they meet lots of friendly people, they learn to like people.

When a kitten is about eight weeks old, it is ready to leave its mother.

Cats that grow
up without getting
used to people
are shy.

These cats are feral. This means they are
half wild. Lots of feral cats live in cities.
They live in little groups and take care
of themselves.

Pet cats normally live for about 12 to 14 years.
The longest a pet cat has ever lived is 34 years.

Cat talk

You can tell how a cat feels by the way it looks and acts.

If a cat rolls onto its back, then it feels safe with you.

Cats stare at each other if they want to fight.
If you blink at a cat, you can make it feel safe.

If a cat wags its tail, leave it alone. It may be feeling angry.

If a cat partly closes its eyes and purrs, it means it feels happy.

If a cat looks at you and says "meow", it wants something.

A cat in danger curves its back to look bigger and scare off its enemy.

Climbing

Cats like to jump and climb. They feel safe in high places.

They have sharp claws that help them hold on as they climb.

12

If a cat falls, it tries to land
on its feet, so it doesn't hurt itself.

As it falls, the cat
twists its head and
front legs around.

Then, the cat
twists its back
legs around.

The cat curves its
back. This helps it
land softly.

Hunting

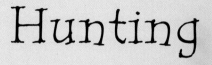

Cats are good hunters.

This pet cat is jumping
to try to catch a bird.

Pet cats are fed
at home, so they
don't need to
hunt for food.

A cat can jump about five times its
own height. How high can you jump?

Wild cats have to hunt for their food.

A hungry wild cat hears a mouse. It crouches down to hide in the grass.

It creeps slowly toward the mouse. The cat's furry paws help it walk very quietly.

When it is close to the mouse, the cat pounces and catches it.

Smells

Cats can smell smells that people can't. They know who other cats are by their smell.

When cats say hello, they sniff each other.

They rub their bodies together to share their smells.

Pet cats rub up against people to say hello, too.

Pet cats scratch things in their owner's house to show it's their home, too.

Cats mark their home area with their smells, so that other cats know it is theirs.

This kitten is rubbing its head on a tree to leave its smell there.

Cross cats

Some cats don't like others being near their home. This is how a cat warns another off.

A black cat comes near an orange cat's home. The orange cat stares hard at it.

The black cat crouches and looks away. This shows it doesn't want to fight.

The black cat creeps away again. The orange cat has won.

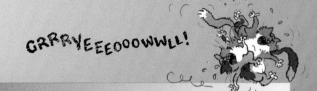

GRRRYEEEOOOWWLL!

Cats hiss, growl and scream when they fight.

Cats don't like fighting. But if they can't warn an enemy off by staring, they might fight.

A cat hisses and then it tries to scratch its enemy with its claws.

Nightlife

Cats like to go out in the evening. They can see in the dark better than people can.

In bright light, a cat's pupils look like slits.

In dim light, a cat's pupils grow big. This lets in any light that's there, so it can see.

A cat's eyes glow if light shines on them when it's dark.

When it's too dark to see, a cat's long whiskers help it feel its way around.

The tips of the cat's whiskers touch the edges of a fence.

The cat knows it can fit through the fence, so it walks through.

Catnap

Cats look for warm, quiet places to sleep.

If it's hot they sleep stretched out.

If it's a little cooler they sleep curled up.

Cats like to sleep. They have lots of quick naps through the day.

This kitten has climbed a tree for a nap.

This cat has just woken up and is stretching.
Stretching helps a cat to wake up and get
ready for action.

A cat spends over half of its life asleep.

Keeping clean

Cats wash themselves to keep clean. Follow the numbers to see how a cat washes itself.

1. The cat licks its paw. It wipes the wet paw on its face.

2. It nibbles its paws to clean dirt off and to tidy its claws.

3. It nibbles at any knots in its fur to get them out.

4. It licks its legs, its whole body and then its tail.

Sometimes cats help to lick each other clean.
This shows they are good friends.

A cat's tongue is very rough. When
a cat licks its fur, its tongue works
like a comb.

Fur

Cats' fur helps keep them warm. Some cats have short fur and some have long, bushy fur.

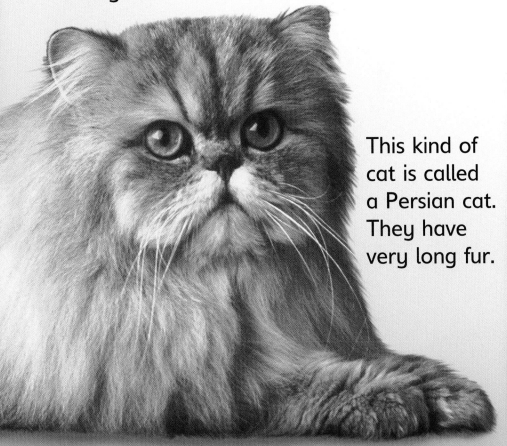

This kind of cat is called a Persian cat. They have very long fur.

In summer, some of a cat's fur falls out, so the cat doesn't get too hot. This is called shedding.

Cats can have different patterns on their fur. Even kittens in the same family can all look different.

Siamese cats have dark ears, faces, tails and paws. They aren't born this way.

The kittens are born pale cream all over.

Later, some parts of their bodies turn dark.

Kinds of cats

There are lots of unusual kinds of pet cats. Different kinds of cats are called breeds.

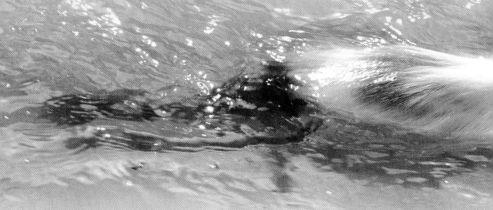

Here are some examples of cat breeds.

Munchkin cats have short legs.

Siamese cats are slim.

Sphynxes have hardly any fur.

This cat is a Turkish Van. Most cats hate water, but Turkish Vans love swimming.

Manx cats have no tails.

Norwegian Forest cats have long, bushy tails.

Most pet cats are a mixture of breeds.

Glossary of cat words

Here are some of the words in this book you might not know. This page tells you what they mean.

 teat - a mother cat has teats on her tummy. Kittens drink milk from them.

 feral - a half-wild animal. Lots of feral cats live in cities or on farms.

 claw - sharp parts on a cat's paws. Claws are an animal's fingernails.

 hunt - to find, chase and kill another animal, usually to eat.

 pupil - the black part in the middle of an animal's or a person's eye.

 nap - a short sleep. Cats nap often, so sometimes naps are called catnaps.

 shedding - losing fur. Cats shed in the summer to keep cool.

Websites to visit

If you have a computer, you can find out more about cats on the Internet. On the Usborne Quicklinks website there are links to four fun websites.

Website 1 - Play a cat game.

Website 2 - Learn more about pet cats and how to take care of them.

Website 3 - Draw a cartoon cat.

Website 4 - Find out about wild cats.

To visit these websites, go to **www.usbornequicklinks.com** and type the keywords "beginners cats". Then click on the link for the website you want to visit. Before you use the Internet, look at the safety guidelines inside the back cover of this book and ask an adult to read them with you.

Index

Acknowledgements

Managing editor: Fiona Watt
Managing designer: Mary Cartwright
Photographic manipulation by Emma Julings

Photo credits
The publishers are grateful to the following for permission to reproduce material:
© **Alamy Images:** 6; © **Ardea London:** 4 (François Gohier), 19 (Pat Morris); © **Corbis:** title (Pat Doyle), 9 (James Marshall), 27 (Julie Habel); © **Getty:** cover (Gary Randall), 12 (Sue Streeter), 21(Desmond Burdon), 26 (Barros & Barros); © **Graeme Teague:** 25; © **ImageState:** 8 (Robert Llewellyn), 22 (Leland Howard), 23 (Veturian); © **Photonica:** 10 (Neo Vision); © **Team Husar:** 7 (Lisa & Mike Husar); © **Warren Photographic:** 14; 3, 17, 20, 28 (Jane Burton); 31 (Jane Burton)

ISBN 0-439-68985-6

12 11 10 9 8 7 6 5 4 3 2 1   5 6 7 8 9 10/0

Printed in the U.S.A.   23

First Scholastic printing, January 2005